REAL LEADERSHIP REAL RESULTS

52 SIMPLE ACTIONABLE LESSONS TO MAKE YOUR LEADERSHIP SHINE

David Suson

REAL LEADERSHIP REAL RESULTS

ISBN: 979-8-218-80627-9

DEDICATION

To my wife, Marilyn, for your unwavering support and belief in me. This book wouldn't exist without you.

And to my friend Quyen, for helping me shape the title and cover. Your insights made this book better.

A NOTE ON HOW TO USE THIS BOOK

Real Leadership, Real Results isn't meant to sit on a shelf. It's designed to be lived. Inside you'll find 52 leadership principles, each paired with a short activity.

Here's how to get the most out of it:

- Think of the book as a year-long journey
- Pick one principle each week
- Do the activity, reflect, and apply it in real life

By the end of 52 weeks, you won't just understand leadership better, you'll *be* even better at it.

This isn't about perfection. It's about progress. One principle, one activity, one week at a time.

To your growth,

David Suson

TABLE OF CONTENTS

INTRODUCTION

Real Leadership Isn't Complicated. It's Just Been Overcomplicated.

If you've ever felt like leadership books are trying to make you memorize a foreign language just to manage a meeting… you're not alone.

For the past few decades, I've been in the trenches leading teams, coaching executives, and speaking to thousands of leaders at workshops, conferences, and retreats. And over and over, I've seen the same problem:

We've made leadership too complex for its own good.

The truth is, most leaders don't need another 400-page theory to memorize. What they need are simple, powerful reminders, guiding principles that work in the real world, where people are messy, time is short, and pressure is high.

That's what this book is.

It's not a manifesto. It's a manual.

A practical, no-fluff, real-talk guide to leadership that actually works because it's built on what *actually matters*.

The Origin: One Model, One Mission

It all started with a single idea: **What if we stopped trying to manage people like they're problems to be solved and started leading them like they matter?**

That question became the foundation for the MVP Model:

Mindset. Value Them. Push Them Up.

You'll find it in Part I, and it's more than a model. It's a mindset shift. It's the heartbeat behind everything I teach, whether I'm on a stage delivering a keynote, coaching a CEO behind closed doors, or helping a manager navigate a tough conversation.

Because when you shift how you *see* leadership…

You change how you *show up* as a leader.

And when you do that, results follow. Every time.

The Middle: Leadership Lessons That Stick

In Part II, we move from the model to the metaphors.

This is where it gets fun.

These are the idioms, simple, memorable phrases that cut through the noise and stick with you when it matters most.

Why idioms? Because people don't remember policies.

They remember moments. Phrases. Stories.

They remember the manager who said, *"You can't turn a cat into a dog,"* and meant it.

They remember the leader who reminded them, *"You're a human, not a robot,"* when they were running on empty.

These idioms aren't fluff, they're flashlights. Each one shines a light on a deeper leadership truth, and comes with a practical activity so you can turn insight into action.

Because great leadership isn't about knowing what to say.

It's about knowing what to do.

The Final Section: How to Show Someone They Matter

You can talk about leadership all day.

But if your people don't feel seen, safe, or significant… it's just talk.

In Part III, you'll find 50 real, tangible ways to show someone they matter.

Not someday. Not "when the timing is right."

But **today**, in a hallway conversation, a one-on-one meeting, or a quick Slack message.

Because here's what I know for sure:

People don't leave companies. They leave leaders.

And they stay for the ones who make them feel like they matter.

So whether you're a CEO, a first-time manager, or just someone who wants to lead better…

This book is for you.

It's meant to be dog-eared, highlighted, and shared.

It's built to help you shine, by helping others shine.

Let's make leadership real again.

Let's make it human.

Let's make it matter.

To your success,

David

PART I

THE MVP MODEL
LEADING PEOPLE LIKE IT MATTERS

In all my years of coaching leaders, interviewing high performers, and building teams that actually *work*, I've come to one unavoidable conclusion: leadership is not about being in charge.

It's about the impact you create through how you show up, how you think, how you see people, and what you're willing to do to help them grow.

Because let's be honest, most leadership advice out there feels like trying to **balance a teacup on the nose of an elephant**. It's overly delicate, too reactive, and just doesn't hold up in the real world. You've got big personalities, complex dynamics, shifting goals, and you're supposed to keep it all steady with checklists and performance reviews?

That's why I developed the MVP model.

Now, this isn't some trendy acronym with seven steps and a trademark symbol. This is a deeply personal, practical framework I've lived and taught for years. And the reason it sticks, why leaders love it, why employees feel it, and why results follow, is because it's built on truth.

MVP stands for: Mindset, Value Them, Push Them Up.

It's simple. But don't mistake that for shallow. MVP goes to the core of how people want to be led, and how leaders actually become great.

If you've heard me speak, you've seen how these three letters crack open a new way of thinking. And if you haven't, you're about to get a front-row seat.

Let's walk through it.

Mindset: It Starts With How You See It

Before you say a word, before you assign a task, before you decide how to lead… it all starts with your mindset.

Your mindset is your lens. It's how you perceive your people, your role, and your responsibility as a leader.

If you see leadership as a chore, you'll lead like it's a burden. You'll look for shortcuts. You'll get annoyed when people don't "just get it." You'll end up with a team that does the bare minimum and resents you in the process.

But if you shift your mindset to this: *Leadership is not about control. It's about unlocking potential.* Then everything changes.

Your tone changes. Your questions change. Your patience increases. Your impact multiplies.

I remember a time in my own career when I realized I had been trying to lead from authority instead of curiosity. I thought people just needed direction, when what they actually needed was belief. Someone to see more in them than they saw in themselves. When I flipped the switch, when I started asking "*How can I help this person grow?*" instead of "*Why aren't you performing?*" that's when my team transformed.

That question **"How can I?"** is the most powerful leadership tool you have. It reframes frustration into possibility. It shifts you from blame to ownership. And it opens the door to creativity, compassion, and real results.

Here's the truth: you can't change people. **You can't turn a cat into a dog.**

But you *can* create an environment where that cat thrives, where they do what they do best, in the way that only they can.

That's what the right mindset does. It helps you see people not through the lens of what *you* want them to be, but for who they *really are*, and who they *could become.*

Value Them: They're People, Not Robots

Let's be honest, this should be obvious. But it isn't.

Too many leaders treat their people like tools to complete tasks. They manage output, not humans. They recognize performance only when it's convenient. And then, they wonder why their team is disengaged.

You cannot fake valuing people. They'll see right through it.

Valuing someone doesn't mean handing out praise like candy. It means noticing the human in front of you. Taking time to understand their world. Listening without distraction. Trusting them with something that matters. Giving feedback because you care, not because it's on your to-do list.

I've interviewed thousands of high performers. You know what they almost *never* say?

"I stayed because the company had a ping-pong table and a free lunch."

But you know what they *do* say?

"I stayed because of my boss. Because they saw something in me. Because they believed in me. Because they made me feel like I mattered."

That's the difference. That's value.

One of the most powerful moments I've seen came from a frontline leader who started every one-on-one meeting with an observation of the employees' impact they had that week.

That leader got more honesty, more insight, and more motivation from their team than any HR program could manufacture. Because people felt seen.

When you value someone, they rise.

When you don't, they eventually leave, or worse, they stay and disengage.

You get what you look for. So look for the good. Find it. Say it. Mean it.

Push Them Up: Real Leaders Build Ladders, Not Thrones

Here's where it gets interesting. Because this is where most managers either freeze… or fly.

"Push them up" doesn't mean push harder. It doesn't mean micromanage, pressure, or nag.

It means you become the *reason* someone grows. You spot potential before they do. You set the bar higher than they've set for themselves. You coach. You support. You challenge, with love and high standards.

A lot of leaders fear this part. They think, *"What if they surpass me?"*

And my answer is always the same: **Then you've succeeded.**

A great leader isn't the star of the show, they're the spotlight operator. Their job is to illuminate others. To help them shine.

There's a story I share about a young employee who was sharp, but hesitant. Her previous boss had torn her down so often she stopped trying. When I worked with her new leader, we rebuilt her confidence step-by-step. It started with assigning small wins, celebrating them, and pushing her just a bit further each time.

Within six months, she was leading meetings, training others, and getting promoted. Not because someone gave her a blueprint, but because someone *pushed her up*.

Think of it like this: if your people were climbing a ladder, are you standing on the next rung, helping them up? Or are you standing at the top yelling down?

Leaders who push others up become unforgettable. Because they give people more than a paycheck, they give them belief, opportunity, and momentum.

MVP In Action: The Multiplier Effect

When you lead with MVP, your team *feels* it.

They perform differently, not because they have to, but because they *want* to. They trust you. They step up. They stay longer. They bring energy instead of excuses.

And they start leading *others* the way you led them.

That's the multiplier effect.

Mindset. Value. Push.

Each part on its own is powerful. But together, they're transformational.

Whether you're leading a team of two or two thousand… whether you're in the C-suite or managing a shift on the floor… MVP is your playbook.

It gives you more than balance. It gives you *stability*, the kind that doesn't collapse the moment pressure hits. No more trying to **balance a teacup on the nose of an elephant**.

Mindset. Value. Push.

That's the foundation. Real leadership. Real results.

Try it. Today. With one person. Change your mindset. Show them value. Push them up.

Watch what happens next.

From Model to Metaphor: The Language of Leadership

You've probably noticed that I like using everyday phrases and metaphors to explain big leadership truths. That's not an accident. These **idioms** aren't just catchy lines. They're memorable shortcuts to the deeper principles I teach on stage and in workshops. They're grounded in the MVP model, and they reinforce everything you just read.

Because let's be honest: leadership is already complicated. If you can remember that *"they're people, not robots,"* or that *"you can't turn a cat into a dog,"* you'll remember to lead with empathy, clarity, and the right expectations.

In the next section, I'm going to unpack some of my favorite idioms, the ones that stick with leaders long after the keynote is over. These are the phrases that teams quote back to me months later, because they're simple… but powerful.

Let's dive into the language of real leadership.

PART II

52 SIMPLE ACTIONABLE LESSONS TO MAKE YOUR LEADERSHIP SHINE

You can't turn a cat into a dog

1. "You can't turn a cat into a dog"

Leadership Principle:

Accept people for who they are, leveraging their strengths rather than trying to change them.

Explanation:

This idiom evokes the humorous image of trying to convince a cat to bark or a dog to purr. Just as animals have distinct traits, people do too, and expecting them to change fundamental aspects of who they are leads to frustration. Great leaders recognize these differences and adapt their approach to leverage individual strengths.

Activity:

Make a list of three team members and identify one unique strength for each. Reflect on how to leverage these traits in your leadership.

They're people not robots

2. "They're people, not robots."

Leadership Principle:

Recognize that employees are human, not machines, and lead with flexibility and understanding.

Explanation:

People aren't programmable devices that can perform flawlessly at the push of a button. Employees bring emotions, vulnerabilities, and quirks to their roles. Effective leaders adapt to their team members' needs, supporting their well-being and appreciating their humanity.

Activity:

Write down three moments this week where you adapted your expectations or actions to accommodate someone's humanity. Reflect on how it improved the outcome.

Balance the teacup on the nose of a dancing elephant

3. "Balance the teacup on the nose of a dancing elephant."

Leadership Principle:

Promote work-life balance and well-being among employees.

Explanation:

Achieving balance amidst life's chaos requires skill and creativity, much like balancing a teacup on a dancing elephant. Helping employees find work-life balance demands intentional effort, and leaders must model this balance themselves to foster a thriving workplace.

Activity:

Reflect on your own work-life balance. Write down one way to model better balance this week, such as leaving work on time or scheduling downtime.

Nobody builds their best ideas inside a suit of armor

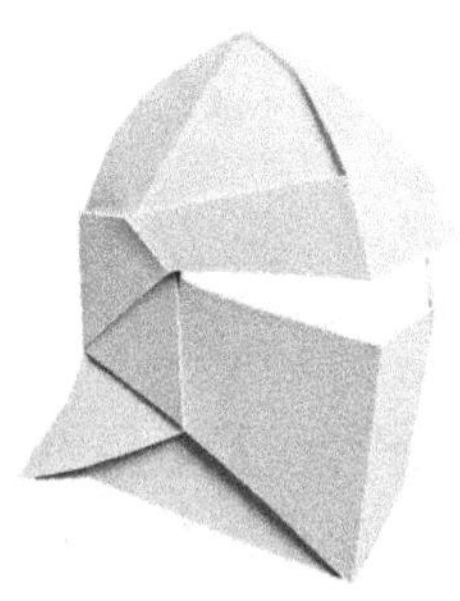

4. "Nobody builds their best ideas inside a suit of armor."

Leadership Principle:

Foster psychological safety, ensuring employees feel comfortable expressing themselves.

Explanation:

When employees feel the need to protect themselves from judgment or criticism, creativity and collaboration are stifled. Leaders who create psychological safety help their team shed this "armor," allowing bold ideas, mistakes, and innovation to emerge.

Activity:

Identify one meeting or situation where someone hesitated to share. Reflect on how you can create a safer environment next time.

Don’t build a rainbow and forget the blue

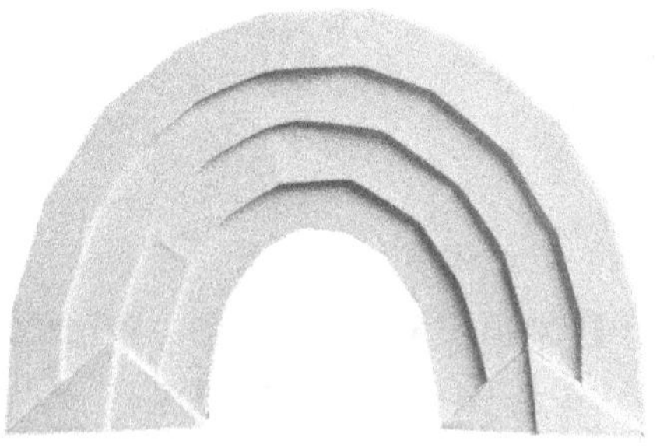

5. "Don't build a rainbow and forget the blue."

Leadership Principle:

Champion diversity and inclusion, creating a workplace where all voices are valued.

Explanation:

A rainbow is incomplete without all its colors, just as a team is diminished when certain voices are excluded. Leaders who embrace diversity create a richer, more innovative workplace.

Activity:

Reflect on one group or perspective you might unintentionally overlook. Write down one way to amplify those voices this week.

Don’t light a lantern and then hide it under the bed.

Inspiration and Purpose

6. "Don't light a lantern and then hide it under the bed."

Leadership Principle:

Inspire through purpose, connecting daily work to a larger vision.

Explanation:

Just as a lantern's purpose is to illuminate, a leader's role is to shine a clear and inspiring vision for their team. Leaders who connect daily work to a greater mission ignite motivation and foster alignment.

Activity:

Write down one way your team's work contributes to the organization's larger goals. Share this insight in your next meeting or conversation.

A kite only flies high when it's tethered to a string

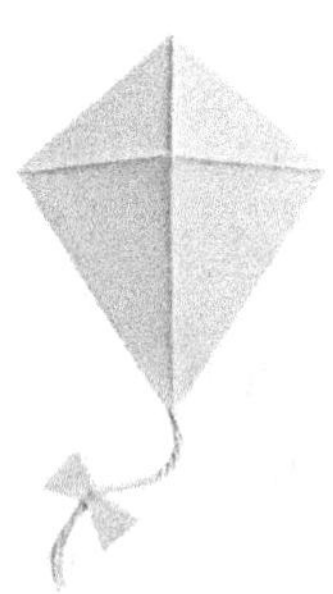

Inspiration and Purpose

7. "A kite only flies high when it's tethered to a string."

Leadership Principle:

Help employees stay grounded while reaching for ambitious goals.

Explanation:

A kite soars because it's tethered, not despite it. Similarly, leaders provide the grounding support employees need to pursue ambitious goals.

Activity:

Identify one ambitious goal your team is pursuing. Write down one way you can provide grounding support, such as clarifying priorities or offering additional resources.

You can’t paint a masterpiece with just one brush

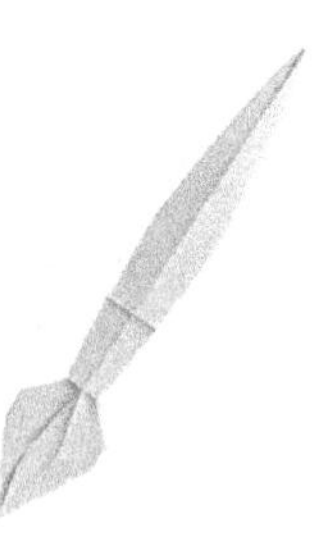

8. "You can't paint a masterpiece with just one brush."

Leadership Principle:

Cultivate diversity of thought and perspective within your team.

Explanation:

A masterpiece requires a variety of tools and colors, just as a team benefits from diverse perspectives and approaches. Encouraging diversity of thought leads to exceptional solutions.

Activity:

Identify one unique "brush" (perspective or skill) that each team member brings. Reflect on how to better incorporate these perspectives into decision-making.

Don’t put the cart before the flying pig

9. "Don't put the cart before the flying pig."

Leadership Principle:

Be realistic about timelines and ensure resources match ambitions.

Explanation:

Achieving ambitious goals requires careful planning and realistic expectations. Leaders must ensure their "cart" (project) has proper support before chasing extraordinary outcomes ("flying pig").

Activity:

Review one current project. Write down one step to ensure realistic expectations or provide additional resources to support its success.

Don’t tie the ship to the shore when it’s meant to sail

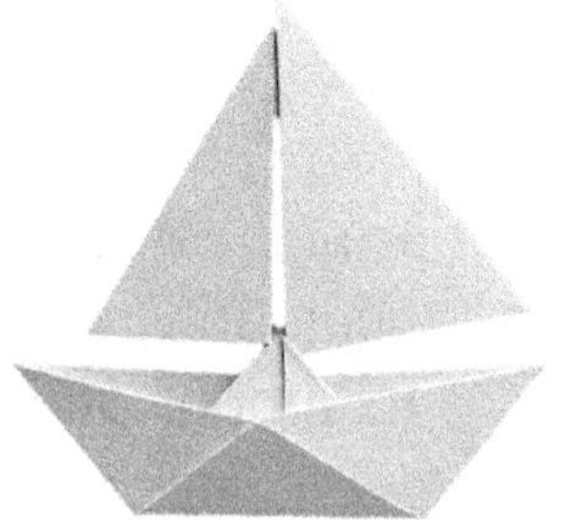

10. "Don't tie the ship to the shore when it's meant to sail."

Leadership Principle:

Encourage autonomy and empower team members to take initiative.

Explanation:

A ship tethered to the dock can't fulfill its purpose of exploring the seas. Similarly, leaders who micromanage stifle their teams. By empowering employees to take ownership, you unleash their potential.

Activity:

Identify one area where you tend to micromanage. Write down one step you'll take this week to delegate and trust your team to handle it.

You can't hold water in a leaky bucket

Trust and Integrity

11. "You can’t hold water in a leaky bucket."

Leadership Principle:

Build trust through consistent follow-through on commitments.

Explanation:

A leaky bucket cannot hold water, just as unreliable leaders cannot retain trust. Consistency and follow-through are essential for building credibility and strong relationships.

Activity:

Write down one promise you’ve made recently. Ensure it’s completed this week, even if it requires extra effort.

Don't sharpen a pencil with a hammer

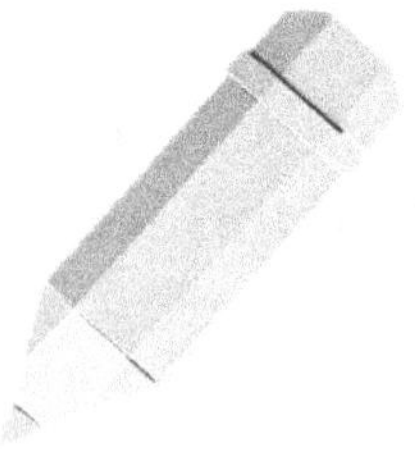

Trust and Integrity

12. "Don't sharpen a pencil with a hammer."

Leadership Principle:

Use the right approach and tone to coach and provide feedback effectively.

Explanation:

Just as a hammer is inappropriate for sharpening a pencil, harsh or misaligned feedback can damage rather than develop employees. Constructive guidance builds confidence and skills.

Activity:

Identify one instance where you'll provide feedback this week. Write down one positive way to frame it constructively.

You can't grow a garden without pulling the weeds

Trust and Integrity

13. "You can't grow a garden without pulling the weeds."

Leadership Principle:

Address issues directly to maintain trust and a healthy culture.

Explanation:

Weeds, like unresolved issues, can choke progress and undermine growth. Tackling problems directly fosters a culture of trust and accountability.

Activity:

Identify one small issue you've been avoiding. Write down one step you'll take this week to address it constructively.

Don’t ask for a map if you’re not willing to follow it

Trust and Integrity

14. "Don't ask for a map if you're not willing to follow it."

Leadership Principle:

Demonstrate consistency between words and actions.

Explanation:

Asking for directions but refusing to follow them is as futile as a leader making promises they don't keep. Consistency inspires trust and credibility.

Activity:

Reflect on one promise or expectation you've set for your team. Ensure your actions this week align with it.

A compass without a needle leaves everyone lost

Trust and Integrity

15. "A compass without a needle leaves everyone lost."

Leadership Principle:

Provide clear direction and consistency in leadership.

Explanation:

A compass without a needle is useless, leaving travelers lost. Similarly, inconsistent leadership leaves teams unfocused. Clear direction ensures alignment and progress.

Activity:

Write down one key priority for your team this week. Reiterate it clearly in your next communication.

You can't teach a fish to climb a tree

16. "You can’t teach a fish to climb a tree."

Leadership Principle:

Leverage individual strengths instead of forcing people into roles that don’t suit them.

Explanation:

This idiom highlights the futility of expecting a fish to succeed at climbing; it’s simply not designed for the task. Similarly, people thrive when their roles align with their natural talents. Great leaders identify individual strengths and position their team members to succeed in roles that play to those strengths.

Activity:

Write down one team member’s unique talent. Think of one way you can better align their role with their strengths this week.

Don't pour soup into a leaky bowl

17. "Don’t pour soup into a leaky bowl."

Leadership Principle:

Provide training and tools to ensure employees can succeed.

Explanation:

This idiom paints a humorous yet frustrating scenario; a leaky bowl can’t hold soup, just as unprepared employees can’t meet expectations. Leaders must invest in equipping their teams with the right tools, training, and resources to thrive. Without this foundation, efforts are wasted, and potential is lost.

Activity:

Identify one resource or skill gap on your team. Write down one step you can take to address it this week, such as sharing an article, arranging training, or providing a tool.

A symphony doesn't happen with just one violin

18. "A symphony doesn't happen with just one violin."

Leadership Principle:

Foster collaboration by encouraging teamwork and valuing every contribution.

Explanation:

A symphony is a collective effort, where each instrument plays a crucial role; no individual can achieve what a well-coordinated group can. Leaders who bring people together harmonize talents to create something extraordinary while ensuring every contribution is valued.

Activity:

Reflect on one team project this week. Write down one way you can encourage collaboration, such as highlighting the value of collective contributions in a meeting.

You can’t send smoke signals in a windstorm

Collaboration and Communication

19. "You can't send smoke signals in a windstorm."

Leadership Principle:

Communicate clearly and effectively to ensure your message isn't lost or misinterpreted.

Explanation:

Unclear or poorly timed communication can lead to confusion and frustration. Leaders who prioritize clarity and intentionality ensure their teams understand and act on the message.

Activity:

Review your next planned communication. Simplify the message into three main points and ensure it's clear and actionable before delivering it.

You can't clap with one hand

20. "You can't clap with one hand."

Leadership Principle:

Encourage open communication and active listening within the team.

Explanation:

Clapping requires two hands working together, just as effective communication requires both speaking and listening. Leaders who foster two-way communication build stronger connections, ensure mutual understanding, and create a more collaborative environment.

Activity:

During your next conversation, focus on listening without interrupting. Write down one key insight you gained from truly listening.

Don’t plant seeds in a garden you never visit

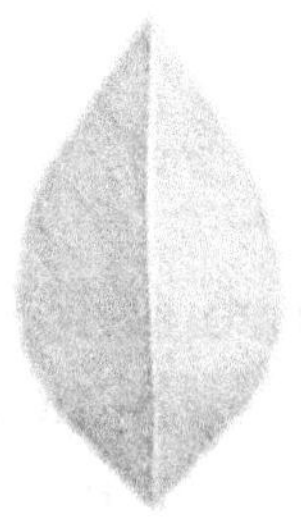

21. "Don't plant seeds in a garden you never visit."

Leadership Principle:

Build trust by being consistently present and engaged with your team.

Explanation:

Planting seeds but neglecting to tend the garden leads to a barren patch, much like sporadic leadership erodes trust. Leaders who regularly check in, support, and show up for their teams cultivate trust and growth over time.

Activity:

Plan one check-in with your team this week, even if informal. Write down one observation or insight you gained from the conversation.

A bridge with missing planks won’t get you across

Collaboration and Communication

22. "A bridge with missing planks won't get you across."

Leadership Principle:

Ensure transparency and honesty in all communications.

Explanation:

A bridge with gaps leaves travelers stranded, just as dishonesty or half-truths weaken trust and hinder progress. Leaders who prioritize transparency build bridges that allow their teams to move forward confidently.

Activity:

Identify one situation where you could be more transparent. Write down one way to communicate more openly this week.

You can't whisper instructions in a thunderstorm

Collaboration and Communication

23. "You can't whisper instructions in a thunderstorm."

Leadership Principle:

Be clear and decisive in high-pressure situations to guide your team effectively.

Explanation:

Whispering in a thunderstorm is futile; it takes clarity and decisiveness to cut through the noise. Similarly, leaders must rise to the occasion in high-pressure situations, providing strong guidance that inspires confidence and action.

Activity:

Think of one challenging situation your team is currently facing. Write down a decisive and clear message you can deliver to provide guidance and focus.

A wheel doesn’t turn with just one spoke

24. "A wheel doesn't turn with just one spoke."

Leadership Principle:

Foster cross-functional collaboration and knowledge-sharing across teams.

Explanation:

A wheel relies on all its spokes to turn smoothly, just as organizations thrive when teams collaborate and share knowledge. Leaders who encourage cross-functional efforts unlock innovation, break down silos, and create a cohesive organization.

Activity:

Identify one area where cross-functional collaboration could be improved. Write down one step you'll take this week to encourage it, such as connecting two teams or facilitating a brainstorming session.

You can't untangle knots by pulling harder

25. "You can't untangle knots by pulling harder."

Leadership Principle:

Approach conflicts with patience and understanding to resolve them effectively.

Explanation:

Pulling harder on a tangled knot only makes it worse, just as forcefully addressing conflict often escalates the problem. Leaders who approach conflicts with care and understanding address root causes and strengthen relationships.

Activity:

Reflect on a recent conflict within your team. Write down one way you could approach it more patiently or empathetically next time.

Don't shout directions from the top of the mountain

26. "Don't shout directions from the top of the mountain."

Leadership Principle:

Lead by example, demonstrating the behaviors you want to see in your team.

Explanation:

People follow leaders who walk beside them, not ones who issue orders from afar. Leading alongside builds trust, respect, and genuine commitment. Walk the talk.

Activity:

Identify one behavior you want your team to adopt. Write down one way you'll model it this week, such as showing punctuality or embracing feedback.

You can't steer a boat if you don't know where the river leads

27. "You can't steer a boat if you don't know where the river leads."

Leadership Principle:

Provide a clear vision and roadmap to keep your team aligned and motivated.

Explanation:

Steering a boat without understanding the river's path leads to aimless drifting. Similarly, leaders who fail to provide a clear vision leave their teams unfocused and unmotivated. By defining the destination and sharing a roadmap, leaders inspire alignment and drive.

Activity:

Write down your team's primary objective for the next quarter. Share it clearly with your team and outline how their roles contribute to achieving it.

You can't outrun a storm, but you can build a better umbrella

Resilience and Adaptability

28. "You can't outrun a storm, but you can build a better umbrella."

Leadership Principle:

Foster resilience by equipping your team to navigate challenges with confidence.

Explanation:

Storms, whether literal or metaphorical, are unavoidable, but leaders can prepare their teams to weather them. By providing tools, support, and encouragement, you empower your team to face adversity with resilience. This idiom emphasizes proactive preparation over avoidance.

Activity:

Identify one challenge your team is currently facing. Write down one way you can help them build resilience, such as sharing a resource or offering encouragement.

A chameleon doesn’t lose its colors by blending in

29. "A chameleon doesn't lose its colors by blending in."

Leadership Principle:

Embrace change and adaptability without compromising core values.

Explanation:

A chameleon's ability to adapt while retaining its core identity is a metaphor for effective leadership during change. Leaders who model flexibility while staying true to their values inspire confidence and encourage adaptability in their teams.

Activity:

Think of one recent change in your organization. Write down one way you can model adaptability while staying true to your principles.

A river doesn't flow straight, but it still reaches the ocean

30. "A river doesn't flow straight, but it still reaches the ocean."

Leadership Principle:

Embrace flexibility and adaptability in pursuit of long-term goals.

Explanation:

Like a river navigating around obstacles, leaders must remain flexible while keeping their eyes on the ultimate destination. This idiom highlights the importance of resilience and creativity in overcoming challenges to achieve long-term success.

Activity:

Think of one challenge or deviation from a plan you faced recently. Write down one lesson you learned and how it will help you adapt moving forward.

You can't knit a sweater with only one thread

31. "You can’t knit a sweater with only one thread."

Leadership Principle:

Value diversity and collaboration as essential elements of success.

Explanation:

A single thread cannot create something as complex as a sweater, just as one perspective alone cannot solve multifaceted challenges. Leaders who weave together diverse skills and viewpoints create stronger, more innovative teams.

Activity:

Identify one perspective or voice you may have overlooked. Write down one way to include it in an upcoming decision or conversation.

Don't tie a balloon to a cinder block

32. "Don't tie a balloon to a cinder block."

Leadership Principle:

Remove unnecessary burdens or obstacles to help your team soar.

Explanation:

A balloon's purpose is to rise, but unnecessary weight holds it down. Similarly, employees thrive when leaders remove barriers that hinder progress. By streamlining processes and addressing inefficiencies, you empower your team to achieve their potential.

Activity:

Identify one obstacle or inefficiency in your team's workflow. Write down one action you can take to remove or mitigate it this week.

An umbrella doesn’t stop the rain, but it keeps you dry

33. "An umbrella doesn't stop the rain, but it keeps you dry."

Leadership Principle:

Be a source of support during challenges, even if you can't fix everything.

Explanation:

Leaders may not be able to prevent every challenge, but they can offer shelter and reassurance. This idiom emphasizes the value of being present and supportive, helping your team weather difficult times with confidence.

Activity:

Think of one challenge your team is currently facing. Write down one way you can offer support, such as providing resources or offering encouragement.

You can't sharpen a blade with a sponge

Resilience and Adaptability

34. "You can't sharpen a blade with a sponge."

Leadership Principle:

Provide constructive feedback and meaningful challenges to help employees grow.

Explanation:

Growth requires the right level of challenge, just as sharpening a blade requires friction, not softness. Leaders who provide honest, constructive feedback and opportunities for development help their teams sharpen their skills and excel.

Activity:

Identify one team member who could benefit from constructive feedback. Write down one way to deliver it effectively this week.

A flashlight without batteries won't light the way

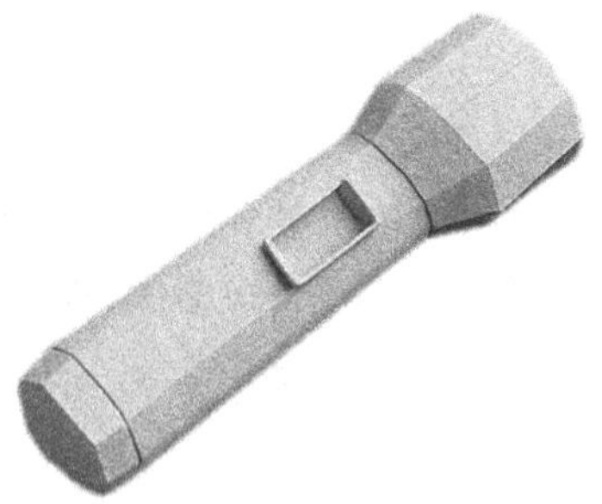

35. "A flashlight without batteries won't light the way."

Leadership Principle:

Provide your team with the energy and resources they need to succeed.

Explanation:

A flashlight is only useful when powered, just as a team needs energy, tools, and resources to perform. Leaders who prioritize equipping their teams ensure they can navigate challenges and achieve success.

Activity:

Identify one resource or tool your team lacks. Write down one way to provide or advocate for it this week.

You can't steer the ship if you're stuck in the crow's nest

Resilience and Adaptability

36. "You can't steer the ship if you're stuck in the crow's nest."

Leadership Principle:

Balance strategic vision with day-to-day engagement to lead effectively.

Explanation:

There is a danger staying too removed from the action. While strategic vision is essential, leaders must also be present and engaged in the day-to-day workings of their teams to guide them effectively.

Activity:

Reflect on how much time you spend on high-level planning versus team engagement. Write down one way to be more present with your team this week.

You can't fly higher if you're always carrying extra baggage

37. "You can’t fly higher if you’re always carrying extra baggage."

Leadership Principle:

Remove unnecessary processes or burdens to help your team focus on what matters.

Explanation:

This idiom captures how excess baggage, like redundant processes or outdated rules, can weigh down a team. Great leaders streamline operations and eliminate obstacles, allowing their teams to focus on meaningful work.

Activity:

Identify one “baggage” or process that feels unnecessary. Write down one step to streamline or eliminate it this week.

Don't build a table with missing legs

38. "Don't build a table with missing legs."

Leadership Principle:

Create an inclusive environment where everyone has a seat at the table.

Explanation:

A table with missing legs is unstable, just as a team lacking inclusion and representation is incomplete. Leaders who ensure that everyone has a seat at the table foster a sense of belonging and create stronger, more collaborative teams. This idiom highlights the importance of valuing all voices.

Activity:

Identify one team member who might feel excluded. Write down one way to invite them to contribute this week.

You can't weave a basket with just one strand

39. "You can't weave a basket with just one strand."

Leadership Principle:

Value collaboration and diverse perspectives as essential elements of success.

Explanation:

A basket requires multiple strands woven together, just as a team benefits from diverse skills, ideas, and viewpoints. Leaders who embrace collaboration and inclusivity create stronger, more innovative solutions.

Activity:

Identify one area where collaboration could be improved. Write down one step you'll take this week to foster it, such as bringing different departments together for a brainstorming session.

A wheel doesn’t turn smoothly if some spokes are too short

Inclusivity and Belonging

40. "A wheel doesn't turn smoothly if some spokes are too short."

Leadership Principle:

Ensure equity and fairness in opportunities and recognition.

Explanation:

A wheel with uneven spokes wobbles, just as inequity in a team creates imbalance and dissatisfaction. Leaders who ensure fairness and recognition across the team foster cohesion and motivation.

Activity:

Reflect on your recent decisions. Write down one action you'll take this week to ensure fairness or equity in your leadership.

Don’t hang a painting in the dark

41. "Don't hang a painting in the dark."

Leadership Principle:

Highlight and celebrate your team's contributions to boost morale and visibility.

Explanation:

A beautiful painting goes unnoticed in the dark, just as great work goes unappreciated without recognition. Leaders who shine a light on their team's efforts build pride and motivation, ensuring that accomplishments are celebrated and seen.

Activity:

Write down one specific accomplishment by a team member. Plan one way to highlight it this week, such as sharing it in a meeting or email.

You can't build a mosaic without all the pieces

42. "You can't build a mosaic without all the pieces."

Leadership Principle:

Embrace the value of individuality and how each person contributes to the whole.

Explanation:

A mosaic's beauty lies in the unique pieces that come together to form a whole. Similarly, teams are strongest when every individual's contribution is valued. Leaders who focus on integrating diverse talents and perspectives create organizations that are richer and more effective.

Activity:

Write down one unique strength for each team member. Reflect on how these strengths contribute to your team's success.

A boat with one oar just goes in circles

43. "A boat with one oar just goes in circles."

Leadership Principle:

Foster mutual accountability and collaboration to move forward.

Explanation:

A boat with only one oar spins endlessly, just as a team without shared responsibility fails to make progress. Leaders who encourage mutual accountability and collaboration align their teams to row together toward shared goals.

Activity:

Identify one area where accountability could be improved. Write down one way you'll encourage shared ownership, such as assigning clear roles for a project.

A bird can't fly with only one wing

44. "A bird can't fly with only one wing."

Leadership Principle:

Balance individual and team needs to create a cohesive workplace.

Explanation:

This idiom captures the importance of balance; a bird relies on both wings to soar, just as teams thrive when individual and collective needs are met. Leaders who balance these priorities create environments where both the team and individuals succeed.

Activity:

Reflect on how you've supported both individual and team goals this week. Write down one action to improve that balance next week.

You can't write a novel with just one word

45. "You can't write a novel with just one word."

Leadership Principle:

Recognize that every person's contribution is necessary for achieving the bigger picture.

Explanation:

A novel requires countless words to tell a story, just as a team's success relies on the contributions of all its members. Leaders who acknowledge the value of each contribution inspire their teams to work together toward shared goals.

Activity:

Think of one way a quieter or less-visible team member contributed this week. Plan how to acknowledge and celebrate their effort.

Every flower dances in the right garden

46. "Every flower dances in the right garden"

Leadership Principle:

Create a supportive environment where individuals can grow and thrive.

Explanation:

Just as flowers need fertile soil to bloom, employees need a supportive and nurturing environment to reach their potential. Leaders who focus on building a positive culture ensure their teams have the foundation for success.

Activity:

Reflect on your team's environment. Write down one change you could make to create a more supportive atmosphere this week.

A tree's roots make the branches strong

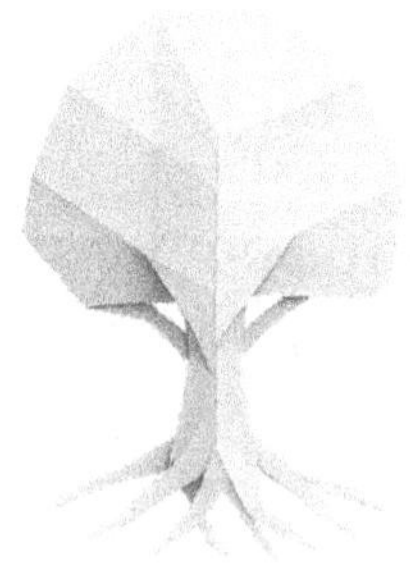

47. "A tree's roots make the branches strong."

Leadership Principle:

Build a foundation of trust and respect to enable growth and success.

Explanation:

A tree's strength lies in its roots, just as a team's resilience depends on trust and respect. Leaders who focus on cultivating these foundational elements create organizations that can weather challenges and grow.

Activity:

Write down one way you've built trust with your team recently. Identify one additional action you can take this week to strengthen those bonds.

You can't navigate the stars without knowing your North Star

48. "You can't navigate the stars without knowing your North Star."

Leadership Principle:

Keep your team aligned with a core purpose or guiding principle.

Explanation:

This idiom emphasizes the importance of a guiding "North Star." Without a clear purpose or principle, it's easy for teams to lose direction. Leaders who consistently communicate their team's guiding mission inspire focus, alignment, and confidence, even amidst uncertainty.

Activity:

Write down one guiding principle for your team. Share it in your next meeting to reinforce alignment.

Don’t chase butterflies when you’re building a hive

49. "Don't chase butterflies when you're building a hive."

Leadership Principle:

Stay focused on strategic goals, avoiding distractions.

Explanation:

This idiom humorously contrasts chasing fleeting opportunities (butterflies) with building something sustainable (a hive). Leaders must prioritize long-term objectives over short-term distractions, ensuring resources and energy are spent on meaningful progress.

Activity:

Write down your team's top three priorities. Reflect on one "distraction" you can let go of this week to stay focused.

A spark is useless without kindling

50. "A spark is useless without kindling."

Leadership Principle:

Cultivate small wins to build momentum toward larger goals.

Explanation:

A spark alone doesn't create a fire, it needs kindling to grow. Similarly, leaders must nurture and celebrate small victories to generate momentum and enthusiasm for larger achievements. This idiom highlights the importance of incremental progress.

Activity:

Identify one "spark" or small win your team achieved this week. Write down one way to celebrate or build on it to keep the momentum going.

Sail by the stars, not the splash

51. "Sail by the stars, not the splash."

Leadership Principle:

Focus on long-term strategy rather than reacting to immediate challenges.

Explanation:

A ship's captain must steer by the stars, not the waves, just as leaders must prioritize long-term goals over short-term distractions. This idiom encourages leaders to maintain focus on the bigger picture, even while navigating daily challenges.

Activity:

Reflect on your team's overarching goals. Write down one action you can take this week to reinforce long-term strategy amidst day-to-day demands.

Don't hang a ladder without the first rung

52. "Don’t hang a ladder without the first rung."

Leadership Principle:

Provide clear steps and guidance to help your team achieve their goals.

Explanation:

A ladder without a bottom rung is inaccessible, just as goals without clear steps are unattainable. Leaders who provide actionable guidance and clear milestones empower their teams to climb higher and succeed.

Activity:

Identify one goal your team is working toward. Write down the next step needed to make progress and communicate it clearly.

PART III

HOW TO SHOW SOMEONE THEY MATTER 50 REAL WAYS TO VALUE AN EMPLOYEE

Great leadership isn't built on grand gestures, it's built on *intentional ones.*

It's the little things done with consistency and sincerity that make people feel safe, seen, and significant. You don't need a budget to value someone. You need awareness. You need empathy. You need to care.

Here are 50 practical, real-world actions you can take to make someone feel valued; not as a cog in a machine, but as a human being with a story, a future, and a heartbeat.

The List:

1. **Ask what they're proud of this week and genuinely listen.** A 90-second question that creates a culture of trust.

2. **Brag about them when they're not in the room.** They'll hear about it, and it'll mean more than if you'd said it directly.

3. **Invite their input before assigning a task.** "Can I get your take on this?" creates ownership, not obligation.

4. **Recognize effort, not just results.** Rewarding the *push* matters just as much as praising the win.

5. **Catch them doing something right.** Most leaders are trained to look for what's broken. Be the one who notices what's working.

6. **Ask how they learn best and adapt when you can.** Training isn't one-size-fits-all. Flexing to their style says: *I see you.*

7. **Let them teach you something.** It flips the power dynamic and shows deep respect.

8. **Give them a challenge just outside their comfort zone.** Stretch them with belief, not pressure.

9. **Say thank you, specifically.** Generic thanks are forgettable. Targeted thanks are remembered.

10. **Ask about their life outside of work and remember what they say.** Simple question. Powerful ripple effect.

11. **Protect their voice in meetings.** If they're being talked over, step in. That one moment can change how safe they feel.

12. **Ask for feedback on your leadership.** It doesn't weaken your authority; it strengthens the relationship.

13. **Trust them with something that matters.** Responsibility says, *I believe in you.*

14. **Offer praise in the moment, not just during reviews.** Catch it, say it, move on. It leaves a mark.

15. **Defend their time.** Be the leader who respects their calendar, not just your own.

16. **Support their growth, even if they outgrow you.** Real leaders create talent that doesn't stay stuck.

17. **Make full eye contact when they speak.** Your presence is the most valuable gift you give.

18. **Follow up on personal updates.** "How did the move go?" shows you were actually listening.

19. **Remember their birthday or any day that matters to them.** Even a short message says, *You matter.*

20. **Tell them they were right.** It builds mutual respect and models humility.

21. **Celebrate the quiet wins.** Some of the best work happens without fanfare.

22. **Be fully present for five uninterrupted minutes.** No devices. No distractions. Just connection.

23. **Let them do it their way, even if yours might be faster.** It shows trust and they might surprise you.

24. **Acknowledge what makes them unique.** "Here's something only *you* bring to this team..."

25. **Pause to give spontaneous encouragement.** Interrupt the grind with fuel, not feedback.

26. **Write a handwritten thank-you note.** It'll end up on their desk, or in their drawer, for a long time.

27. **Recognize growth, not just performance.** "You've come a long way in how you handle pressure." That's gold.

28. **Give credit freely.** Especially if you played a role. Shine the light outward.

29. **Create opportunities for them to shine.** Let them lead a presentation, pitch a client, or share their idea.

30. **Apologize when you mess up.** It doesn't weaken your leadership, it deepens their trust.

31. **Avoid sarcasm.** It's not as harmless as it seems. Clear is kind.

32. **Coach privately, praise publicly.** It's a rule for a reason.

33. **Check in with no agenda.** "How are you really doing this week?" Sincerely.

34. **Let them shape decisions.** Input turns into investment.

35. **Make some conversations about *them*, not their tasks.** They aren't just a to-do list.

36. **Clear roadblocks for them.** Your job isn't to do their job, it's to make it doable.

37. **Tell them what you *see* in them.** Not what they *do*. Who they *are*.

38. **Deliver tough feedback with dignity.** You can be honest without being harsh.

39. **Invite them to mentor or teach someone else.** It shows: *I trust you to lead, not just follow.*

40. **Say, "I'm glad you're here."** It lands deeper than you think.

41. **Respect their boundaries.** Pushing past them doesn't drive performance, it drives people away.

42. **Ask about their family and follow up.** "How's your mom doing?" can mean everything in a hard week.

43. **Celebrate their life moments.** New baby. New degree. New chapter. Celebrate *them.*

44. **Offer flexibility when life throws curveballs.** Empathy beats efficiency in the long run.

45. **Acknowledge the hard stuff they're dealing with.** "I know things are tough right now. I've got your back."

46. **Ask what lights them up outside of work.** Their eyes will tell you more than their words.

47. **Respect how they decompress.** Introverts and extroverts recharge differently. Don't assume.

48. **Honor the way they communicate.** Some people need time to think. Some need to talk it out. Adjust accordingly.

49. **Ask about their goals beyond the job.** Not everyone wants to climb the ladder. Some want to build their own.

50. **Tell them you care through tone, time, and truth.** You don't need the perfect words. Just the real ones.

<u>BONUS #51</u>: Coach them to improve using LB and NT

> **LB** tells them what you liked best about what they did.
> **NT** tells them what to do next time to get even better.
>
> Think of it this way, if they performed at a 7 on a scale of 1 to 10. What did they do to earn the 7? What do they need to do next time to move up even 1 or 2, or to move to a 10?

> This is a positive coaching technique. It will take some time but eventually employees will look forward to your feedback because it will make them even better.

You don't have to do all 51.

But pick a few and make them a habit.

Because when someone feels safe, trusted, and valued… they don't just show up.

They bring their best. They solve bigger problems. They stay longer.

And they start leading others the same way you led them.

That's what real leadership does.

It multiplies.

CONCLUSION

Leadership isn't about knowing it all.
It's about caring enough to show up, to keep learning, and to lead like people matter.

If this book has reminded you of anything, I hope it's this:
You don't need a title to lead.
You don't need a perfect plan.
You don't need permission.

What you need is a mindset, a belief that how you show up *matters*.

To your team.
To your company.
To the people who look to you when things are uncertain.

You've now got the tools, the model, the metaphors, the moments.
Use them.
Test them.
Make them your own.

Start with one person.
See them.
Value them.
Push them up.

Because when one leader leads this way, it changes a team.
When a team leads this way, it changes a culture.
And when enough people lead this way, it changes everything.

Let's stop chasing perfect leadership.
Let's start choosing **real** leadership.
The kind that leaves people better.
The kind that gets results.
The kind that multiplies.

If this message resonates, and you want to bring this kind of leadership to your organization, I'd be honored to help. Whether through a keynote that sparks change, a workshop that builds momentum, or coaching that transforms how your leaders lead…

Let's start a conversation.

Visit **DavidSuson.com** to learn more, check availability, or reach out directly.

Let's make leadership real again.
Let's make it human.
Let's make it matter.

To your success,

David

ABOUT DAVID SUSON

David Suson is a sought-after keynote speaker and executive coach who has helped thousands of leaders unlock higher performance through practical, real-world strategies. With decades of experience leading teams and training organizations, from Fortune 500 companies to fast-growing startups, David's insights are trusted, engaging, and immediately actionable. Known for his powerful stories, sharp humor, and ability to cut through the noise, David helps leaders build influence, drive accountability, and create lasting change. To bring David's transformative message to your event or team, visit DavidSuson.com.

Email: david@davidsuson.com

Website: www.DavidSuson.com

Reviews and Demo Reel: www.talkadot.com/s/david

WORK WITH DAVID SUSON

Bring Real Leadership to Your Organization

If this book resonated with you and you're ready to turn these ideas into action, I'd love to help.

I work with organizations of all sizes to spark meaningful leadership change through:

- **Keynotes** that inspire your audience and shift mindsets
- **Workshops** that build practical skills and team alignment
- **Executive Coaching** that drives personal growth and performance
- **Long-Term Programs** that transform culture and results from the inside out

Whether you're navigating change, developing your managers, or building a culture where people thrive, I can help your team lead like it matters.

Let's start with a conversation.

Learn more or inquire at: DavidSuson.com

Reviews, feedback and speaking reels at: talkadot.com/s/david

Or email me directly at **david@davidsuson.com**

www.ingramcontent.com/pod-product-compliance
Lightning Source LLC
LaVergne TN
LVHW020635100826
845148LV00012B/2189
9798218806279